JERM
STR
TH

Something in the Air

by Peter Gill

Something in the Air was first performed at Jermyn Street Theatre, London, on 13 October 2022.

cast

Colin	**IAN GELDER**
Alex	**CHRISTOPHER GODWIN**
Clare	**CLAIRE PRICE**
Nicholas	**JAMES SCHOFIELD**
Gareth	**SAM THORPE-SPINKS**
Andrew	**ANDREW WOODALL**

production team

Writer	**PETER GILL**
Director	**PETER GILL & ALICE HAMILTON**
Set & Costume Designers	**ANETT BLACK & NEIL IRISH**
Lighting Designer	**JAMIE PLATT**
Sound Designer	**HARRY BLAKE**
Assistant Director	**SAM WOOF**
Production Manager	**LUCY MEWIS-McKERROW**
Deputy Stage Manager	**HEATHER SMITH**
Rehearsal Room Stage Manager	**RICKY McFADDEN**
Assistant Stage Manager	**LILY BROWN**
Production Technician	**TOM McCREADIE**
Production Carpenter	**ADAM SMITH**
Scenic Artists	**EMILY CARNE &**
	MARY MACKEN ALLEN
Intern Production Manager	**ANNABELLE LAMB**
Photographer	**STEVE GREGSON**
Videographer	**RORY CHAMBERS**
PR	**DAVID BURNS**

Thanks to Stuart Thompson, Stephen Rashbrook, Henry Everett, Rachel Pickup, David Beames, Stanley Morgan, Riverside Studios, Edward Callow, Mel Kenyon.

Special thanks to our former Artistic Director and Executive Producer, Tom Littler.

cast

Ian Gelder Colin

Theatre includes: *The Model Apartment*, *Racing Demon* (Theatre Royal Bath); *The March on Russia*, *Definitely the Bahamas* (Orange Tree Theatre); *The Treatment* (Almeida Theatre); *Human Animals*, *The Low Road*, *Fire Face* (Royal Court Theatre); *Company*, *Racing Demon* (Sheffield Crucible); *Precious Little Talent* (Trafalgar Studios); *Lingua Franca* (Finborough Theatre); *The Power of Yes*, *Henry IV Part 1 & 2*, *His Dark Materials*, *Stuff Happens* (National Theatre); *The Crucible*, *Taming of the Shrew*, *Richard III*, *Titus Andronicus*, *The Merchant of Venice* (Royal Shakespeare Company); *Three Sisters* (Chichester Festival Theatre).

Television includes: *Fifteen-Love* (World Productions/Amazon); *Doctor Who*, *Casualty*, *Queers – I Miss The War*, *EastEnders*, *Psychoville*, *Silent Witness*, *Holby City*, *My Dad's the Prime Minister*, *Hawkins*, *Absolutely Fabulous*, *The Day Today*, *Skallagrigg*, *Blackeyes* (BBC); *Lore* (Amazon Studios); *Snatch* (Little Island Pictures); *Riviera* (Archery Pictures); *Game of Thrones* (HBO/Sky); *Mr Selfridge*, *Endeavour*, *Fallen Angel*, *The Bill*, *Kavanagh QC* (ITV).

Film includes: *Surge*, *Little Dorritt*, *The Fool*, *Johnny Loves Suzy*, *Jinnah*, *The Emissary*, *Pope Joan*.

Christopher Godwin Alex

Theatre includes: *A Christmas Carol* (Nottingham Playhouse); *Better Off Dead* (Stephen Joseph Theatre); *Amadeus*, *This House* (National Theatre); *The Crucible* (Old Vic Theatre); *Versailles* (Donmar Warehouse); *The Two Merchants of Modena*, *A Midsummer Nights Dream*, *The City Madam*, *Cardenio*, *The Canterbury Tales* (Royal Shakespeare Company); *Henry IV Part I*, *Henry IV Part II*, *Love's Labour's Lost* (Shakespeare's Globe); *Sherlock's Last Case* (Watermill Theatre); *A Midsummer Night's Dream*, *Henry IV Part I*, *As You Like It*, *Romeo and Juliet* (Regent's Park Open Air Theatre).

Television includes: *Anatomy of a Scandal* (Netflix); *The Miniaturist*, *My Family*, *Land Girls: Forgotten Army*, *Breaking the Mould*, *After You've Gone*, *Lead Balloon*, *Waking the Dead*, *Crisis Command/The Bunker*, *Murder in Mind III: Contract*, *Casualty*, *Manchild II*, *Strange* (BBC); *Harley and the Davidsons* (Discovery Channel); *The Hollow Crown II* (Shakespeare Productions Ltd); *A Young Doctor's Notebook* (Big Talk Productions); *Dark Matters 2* (Wide Eyes Entertainment); *The Bill* (Talkback Thames).

Film includes: *The Dig*, *Emma*, *Mary Poppins Returns*, *The Darkest Day*, *Scoop*, *Blackball*, *The Avengers*, *A Handful of Dust*, *Porridge*.

Claire Price Clare

Theatre includes: *Raya*, *Private Lives* (Hampstead Theatre); *Taming of the Shrew/ Measure for Measure*, *Volpone*, *Don Carlos*, *Brand* (Royal Shakespeare Company); *King Lear* (Duke of York's Theatre); *Poison* (Orange Tree Theatre); *Things We Do* for Love (Bath Theatre Royal); *The Winter's Tale*, *The Daughter-in-Law*, *Company*, *The Pride*, *Richard III*, *The Tempest*, *Much Ado About Nothing* (Sheffield Crucible Theatre); *Way of the World* (Chichester Festival Theatre); *Little Platoons* (The Bush Theatre); *The Power of Yes* (National Theatre).

Television includes: *Call the Midwife* (Neal Street Productions); *Home Fires*, *Home Fires II* (ITV); *Capital* (Kudos); *The Coroner*, *The Outcast*, *Doctors*, *Murder in Mind: Sleeper*, *Out of This World*, *Whistleblower*, *Daziel & Pascoe* (BBC); *Apparitions* (Lime Pictures Ltd); *London's Burning* (LWT).

Film includes: *The Second Best Exotic Marigold Hotel*, *Jump*, *Hereafter*, *Cuckoo*, *Solo Shuttle*.

James Schofield Nicholas

Theatre includes: *Shakespeare in Love* (The Living Theatre); *The History Boys* (Wolverhampton Grand Theatre).

Television includes: *Ackley Bridge* (The Forge Entertainment).

Film includes: *Death on the Nile*, *The Courier.*

Sam Thorpe-Spinks Gareth

Theatre includes: *The Jew* (Kiln Theatre); *Barbarians* (Filter Theatre); *Faceless* (Park Theatre).

Television includes: *Sexy Beast* (Paramount); *A Spy Amongst Friends* (Sony/ Spectrum); *Is This Sexual Harassment?* (BBC).

Sam recently graduated from from Guildhall School of Music & Drama.

Andrew Woodall Andrew

Theatre includes: *Bloody Difficult Women* (Riverside Studios); *Admissions* (Trafalgar Studios); *Antony and Cleopatra*, *Julius Caesar*, *Wendy and Peter Pan* (Royal Shakespeare Company); *First Light* (Chichester Festival Theatre); *The Wars of the Roses* (Rose Theatre Kingston); *Great Britain*, *Women Beware Women*, *The Voysey Inheritance*, *The Life of Galileo*, *Luther*, *The Shape of the Table*, *Racing Demon* (National Theatre); *The Browning Version/South Downs* (Harold Pinter Theatre); *Benefactors* (Sheffield Crucible).

Television includes: *Endeavour* (Mammoth); *The Reckoning*, *Lucan*, *Grantchester*, *The Suspicions of Mr Whicher* (ITV); *Lockwood and Co* (Big Talk/Complete Fiction); *Des* (Mud Productions); *New Worlds* (Company Pictures); *An Adventure in Space and Time*, *Miranda*, *Silk* (BBC).

Film includes: *Where is Anne Frank*, *Solo: A Star Wars Story*, *303 Squadron*, *The Riot Club*, *Belle*, *Johnny English Reborn*, *Count of Monte Cristo*, *Regeneration.*

production team

Peter Gill Writer & Director

Peter Gill was born in 1939 in Cardiff and started his professional career as an actor. A director as well as a writer, he has directed over a hundred productions in the UK, Europe and North America. At the Royal Court Theatre in the sixties, he was responsible for introducing D. H. Lawrence's plays to the theatre. The founding director of Riverside Studios and the National Theatre Studio, Peter Gill lives in London. His plays include *The Sleepers Den* (Royal Court, London, 1965), *A Provincial Life* (Royal Court, 1966), *Over Gardens Out* (Royal Court, 1968), *Small Change* (Royal Court, 1976), *Kick for Touch* (National Theatre, London, 1983), *Cardiff East* (National Theatre, 1997), *Certain Young Men* (Almeida Theatre, London, 1999), *The York Realist* (English Touring Theatre, 2001), *Original Sin* (Sheffield Crucible, 2002), *Another Door Closed* (Theatre Royal, Bath, 2009), *A Provincial Life* (National Theatre of Wales, Sherman Cymru, Cardiff, 2011), *Versailles* (Donmar Warehouse, London, 2014) and *As Good a Time as Any* (Print Room at the Coronet, 2015).

Alice Hamilton Director

Theatre includes: *The Memory of Water*, *The Dumb Waiter* (Hampstead Theatre); *Paradise* and *Every Day I Make Greatness Happen* (Hampstead Downstairs); *Blood Wedding* (Salisbury Playhouse); *The Weatherman* (Park Theatre); *In Lipstick* (Pleasance Theatre); *While We're Here* (Bush); *Echo's End* (Salisbury Playhouse); *Orca* (Papatango); *Thirty Christmases* (Supporting Wall); *German Skerries* (Orange Tree/tour); *Eventide* (Arcola/tour); *Visitors* (Bush /Arcola/tour); *Orson's Shadow* (Southwark Playhouse); *Fear of Music* (Up in Arms/Out of Joint tour) and *At First Sight* (Latitude Festival/tour).

She has directed a short film *Needletail* written by Barney Norris, starring Linda Bassett, Robin Soans and David Beames.

She worked as Staff Director on *Man and Superman* at the National Theatre, and has directed development workshops and rehearsed readings with the Royal Court, National Theatre, Salisbury Playhouse and High Tide.

Neil Irish Set & Costume Designer

For Jermyn Street Theatre: *The Tempest*, *All's Well That Ends Well* (also Guildford Shakespeare Company), *Anything That Flies*, *First Episode*.

Theatre includes: *Hamlet*, *Macbeth*, *Measure for Measure*, *Romeo and Juliet*, *The Two Gentlemen of Verona*, *Julius Caesar*, *Much Ado About Nothing*, *The Winter's Tale*, *The Taming of the Shrew*, *King Lear*, *Twelfth Night*, *Othello*, *As You Like It*, *A Midsummer Night's Dream*, *The Merchant of Venice*, *Richard III* (Guildford Shakespeare Company); *The Nutcracker* (Reading); *Forever Young* (W11 Opera); *One Man Two Guvnors* (tour); *A Christmas Carol*, *Peter Pan*, *Hansel & Gretel*, *Betrayal*, *Alice in Wonderland* (Derby); *Dishoom* (Rifco Theatre Co/Watford Palace); *Carmen*

(English Touring Opera Spring Tour); *Dr Miracle*, *Carmen* (Royal Academy of Music); *Così fan tutte* (Guildhall Opera); *Carmen* (New Zealand Opera); *Jekyll and Hyde* (Frankfurt); *House & Garden*, *Peter Pan*, *Alice in Wonderland* (Watermill Theatre); *Don Giovanni*, *Barber of Seville*, *Madam Butterfly*, *Ill Trittico* (Opera Holland Park); *Tommy* (UK tour); *Le Centerentola* (Danish National Opera/Opera Holland Park); *A Tale of Two Cities* (Hong Kong/Edinburgh Fringe Festival); *Look Back In Anger* (60th Anniversary UK tour); *The Shape of Things* (Atak Theatre, Istanbul); *Boy With A Suitcase* (Arcola Theatre); *Agamemnon*, *Prometheus*, *Frogs* (Cambridge Arts); *Woyzeck* (Gate/St Anne's Theatre, New York); *Rodelinda and Amadigi* (Dublin/BAM New York); *Jekyll and Hyde* (Hong Kong/London).

Neil trained at Birmingham and later, at The Slade School of Art UCL. He has also worked for both Set and Costume Departments for BBC TV.

Anett Black Set & Costume Designer

For Jermyn Street Theatre: *Love All*, *The Tempest*, *A Christmas Carol* and *All's Well That Ends Well* (both also Guildford Shakespeare Company).

Theatre includes: *Hamlet*, *Macbeth*, *King Arthur*, *Much Ado About Nothing*, *Romeo and Juliet*, *Julius Caesar*, *King Lear*, *Othello* (Guildford Shakespeare Company); *The Trials of Oscar Wilde* (Theatre Royal Windsor); *Jekyll and Hyde*, *Pygmalion*, *The Picture of Dorian Grey* (EuropeanArts, Trafalgar Studios/Italian tour); *Christmas Carol* (UK tour); *The Bacchae* (National Trust); *Pippin*, *9 to 5*, *Hair*, *The Fix*, *Blood Wedding*, *Our Country's Good* (Bellairs Theatre); *Bittergirls* (King's Head); *The Promise* (Elizabeth Hall London); *For Ever Young*, *The Price* (Hammersmith); *Antigone* (Spruce Wood).

Jamie Platt Lighting Designer

Lighting designs include: *The Last Five Years* (West End); *Jellyfish* (National Theatre); *Word-Play* (Royal Court Theatre); *Kes* (Octagon Theatre & Theatre by the Lake); *Kinky Boots* (New Wolsey Theatre); *The Barber of Seville* (Nevill Holt Opera); *RIDE*, *Mythic* (Charing Cross Theatre); *Anna Karenina* (Silk St. Theatre); *Either*, *Paradise*, *Yous Two* (Hampstead Theatre); *SUS*, *Never Not Once*, *Gently Down The Stream*, *Alkaline* (Park Theatre); *Moonlight and Magnolias* (Nottingham Playhouse); *The Last Five Years*, *Beast*, *Klippies* (Southwark Playhouse); *Le Grand Mort* (Trafalgar Studios); *Cracked*, *Remembrance* (Old Vic Theatre); *Absurd Person Singular* (Watford Palace Theatre); *The Beat of our Hearts* (Northcott Theatre); *Singin' in the Rain* (The Mill at Sonning); *Sonny*, *Once On This Island* (ArtsEd); *Blood Orange*, *The Moor*, *Where Do Little Birds Go?* (Old Red Lion Theatre); *Checkpoint Chana*, *Quaint Honour*, *P'yongyang*, *We Know Where You Live*, *Chicken Dust* (Finborough Theatre); *Paper Cut*, *Reared*, *Screwed*, *Grey Man* (Theatre503).

Associate lighting designs include: *Frozen*, *SIX* (West End & international); *INK*, *The Night of the Iguana*, *The Starry Messenger*, *Bitter Wheat* (West End); *Albion*, *The Hunt*, *Three Sisters*, *Machinal* (Almeida Theatre).

Jamie's award nominations include Knight of Illumination Award, BroadwayWorld Award and Five OffWestEnd Awards for Best Lighting Design.

Harry Blake Sound Designer

Theatre includes: *Say Yes to Tess* (Leeds Playhouse); *The Memory of Water* (Hampstead Theatre); *Captain Corelli's Mandolin* (Harold Pinter Theatre and national tour); *Wild East* (Young Vic); *Thor and Loki* (HighTide); *The March on Russia* (Orange Tree Theatre); *Ode to Leeds*, *Rudolf* (West Yorkshire Playhouse); *Blush* (Soho Theatre and tour); *Her Naked Skin*, *Night Must Fall*, *Hedda Gabler*, *BIKE* (Salisbury Playhouse); *Septimus Bean*, *Jason and the Argonauts*, *The Snow Child* (Unicorn); *MEGABALL* (National Theatre Let's Play); *Rapunzel* (Cambridge Junction); *The Secret Seven*, *The Beggar's Opera* (Storyhouse Chester); *The Graduate* (Leicester Curve and tour); *Manga Sister*, *Rhinegold* (The Yard); *The Island Nation* (Arcola Theatre); *Casa Valentina* (Southwark Playhouse); *P'yongyang* (Finborough Theatre); *To Dream Again* (Theatr Clwyd).

Sam Woof Assistant Director

Theatre includes: As Writer/Director: *Don't Shoot the Albatross* (Golden Goose Theatre); *With One Eye Open: Shostakovich and Other Insomniacs* (Pilch Theatre); *Sex with Friends and other tiny catastrophes* (North Wall Arts Centre, Pleasance Edinburgh, winner of the Musical Theatre Review's Special Award at the Edinburgh Fringe). As Director: *Merrily We Roll Along* (Oxford Playhouse); *Crave* (Pilch Theatre). As Assistant Director: *Enron* (Oxford Playhouse). As Composer: *Don't Say Macbeth* (Zoo Playground); *Fine Thanks: A Verbatim Musical* (Savoy Theatre).

Sam Woof is a theatre-maker based in London. They studied at the University of Oxford and are currently undertaking a masters degree in directing at Birkbeck College London.

A small theatre with big stories

Jermyn Street Theatre is a hidden gem. It combines the comfort and convenience of the West End with the intimacy of a studio. Every seat has a perfect view of the stage, and even a whisper is audible. Every seat is a premium seat.

Our tiny bar offers a selection of soft and alcoholic refreshments.

Piccadilly Circus and Leicester Square are moments away, and the restaurants, galleries and bookshops of St James's are on our doorstep. This is a secret theatre in the heart of the West End – once found, never forgotten.

In 1994, Howard Jameson and Penny Horner discovered the space, and raised the money to convert it into a beautiful theatre. Since then we have staged hundreds of plays and musicals, winning countless awards. Many productions have transferred in London or to Broadway.

This is where careers ignite, where playwrights take risks, where great actors perform just feet away from the audience. This is where magic happens.

our friends

Our friends are at the heart of our theatre.

We have only 70 seats, which makes attending our theatre a magical experience. But even if we sell every seat, we still need to raise more funds.

If you think you could help support our theatre, then please visit www.jermynstreettheatre.co.uk/friends/

Director's Circle
Anonymous
Michael & Gianni Alen-Buckley
Judith Burnley
Philip Carne MBE and Christine Carne
Jocelyn Abbey & Tom Carney
Colin Clark RIP
Lynette & Robert Craig
Flora Fraser
Charles Glanville & James Hogan
Crawford & Mary Harris
Judith Johnstone
Ros & Duncan McMillan
Leslie & Peter MacLeod-Miller
James L. Simon
Marjorie Simonds-Gooding
Peter Soros & Electra Toub
Melanie Vere Nicoll
Robert Westlake & Marit Mohn

—————————————

The Miranda Club
Anonymous
Anthony Ashplant
Derek Baum
Geraldine Baxter
Gyles & Michèle Brandreth
Anthony Cardew
Tim Cribb
Sylvia de Bertodano
Janie Dee
Anne Dunlop
Nora Franglen
Robert & Pirjo Gardiner
Mary Godwin

Louise Greenberg
Ros and Alan Haigh
Phyllis Huvos
Frank Irish
Marta Kinally
Yvonne Koenig
Hilary King
Jane Mennie
Charles Paine
John & Terry Pearson
Iain Reid
Martin Shenfield
Carol Shephard-Blandy
Jenny Sheridan
Brian Smith
Dana-Leigh Strauss
Mark Tantam
Brian & Esme Tyers
Jatinder Verma

—————————————

The Ariel Club
Richard Alexander
David Barnard
Martin Bishop
Katie Bradford
Nigel Britten
Christopher Brown
Donald Campbell
James Carroll
Ted Craig
Jeanette Culver
Valerie Dias
Robyn Durie
Shomit Dutta
Maureen Elton
Anthony Gabriel

Carol Gallagher
Roger Gaynham
Paul Guinery
Diana Halfnight
Julie Harries
Andrew Hughes
Margaret Karliner
David Lanch
Keith Macdonald
Vivien Macmillan-Smith
Kate and John Peck
Adrian Platt
A J P Powell
Oliver Prenn
Martin Sanderson
Nicholas Sansom
Andrew WG Savage
Nigel Silby
Bernard Silverman
Anthony Skyrme
Philip Somervail
Robert Swift
Paul Taylor
Gary Trimby
Kevin Tuffnell
Ian Williams
Marie Winckler
John Wise

Something in the Air

Peter Gill was born in 1939 in Cardiff and started his professional career as an actor. A director as well as a writer, he has directed over a hundred productions in the UK, Europe and North America. At the Royal Court Theatre in the sixties, he was responsible for introducing D. H. Lawrence's plays to the theatre. The founding director of Riverside Studios and the National Theatre Studio, Peter Gill lives in London. His plays include *The Sleepers Den* (Royal Court, London, 1965), *A Provincial Life* (Royal Court, 1966), *Over Gardens Out* (Royal Court, 1968), *Small Change* (Royal Court, 1976), *Kick for Touch* (National Theatre, London, 1983), *Cardiff East* (National Theatre, 1997), *Certain Young Men* (Almeida Theatre, London, 1999), *The York Realist* (English Touring Theatre, 2001), *Original Sin* (Sheffield Crucible, 2002), *Another Door Closed* (Theatre Royal, Bath, 2009), *A Provincial Life* (National Theatre of Wales, Sherman Cymru, Cardiff, 2011), *Versailles* (Donmar Warehouse, London, 2014) and *As Good a Time as Any* (Print Room at the Coronet, 2015).

PETER GILL

Something in the Air

faber

First published in 2022
by Faber and Faber Limited
74–77 Great Russell Street
London WC1B 3DA

Typeset by Brighton Gray
Printed and bound in the UK by CPI Group (Ltd), Croydon CR0 4YY

A CIP record for this book
is available from the British Library

978-0-571-38145-6

2 4 6 8 10 9 7 5 3 1

Something in the Air was first performed at Jermyn Street Theatre, London, on 13 October 2022, with the following cast:

Colin Ian Gelder
Alex Christopher Godwin
Clare Claire Price
Nicholas James Schofield
Gareth Sam Thorpe-Spinks
Andrew Andrew Woodall

Directors Peter Gill and Alice Hamilton
Set and Costume Designers Anett Black and Neil Irish
Lighting Designer Jamie Platt
Sound Designer Harry Blake
Assistant Director Sam Woof

Characters

Alex
late seventies

Colin
late seventies

Gareth
early twenties

Nicholas
early twenties

Andrew
late forties

Clare
late forties

SOMETHING IN THE AIR

It might be easier
  To fail with land in sight,
Than gain my blue peninsula
  To perish of delight.

Emily Dickinson

What would it be to start life again and to know
that one was doing so. What would it be if our life
now, the life we've already lived that is – what if
that was, as it were, a rough sketch and the other a
clean sheet. Then each of us, I think, would try,
above all, try to create the right setting for his life.
Create for himself surroundings like these. A house
like this, filled with flowers and full of light.

Anton Chekhov, *Three Sisters*
(in a version by Peter Gill)

Alex and Colin are sitting next to each other in identical wing-backed chairs. Alex stage left, Colin stage right. Alex has a knitted rug over his knees and they are holding hands unobtrusively, not much more than touching.

Colin (*adjusting Alex's rug*) Alright . . . ?

   Alex makes a sound in reply.

Are you?

   Alex makes a similar sound.

Colin (*imitating and chuckling*) Yes?

Alex Yes.

Colin Yes.

Alex Aye.

Colin Good, good.

   Ad lib. Laughter.

There we are.

Alex The first time I came to see you, in Hammersmith, the tide was so high on the river that there were sandbags stacked against the wall to prevent a breach. I came out of the station, as you said, and crossed under the spars of the new flyover they were building. And as I walked down by the side of the mansion flats at the side of the bridge, I could see the sandbags piled right up, and, when I got nearer, that there was water leaking through the wooden boards that plugged a gap in the wall giving the first boathouse access to the river. The pontoon was riding so high that the level was inches away from the top but quite still. On the other bank, the towpath under the bridge was flooded, with the poplars nearby skirted in water. And nothing it seemed moving.

Colin Do you want anything?

Alex What?

Colin Do you?

Alex No. No.

Colin Sure?

Alex Yes.

Colin Tell me if you do, yes?

Alex I will.

Colin If you want anything will you, eh? Eh?

Alex Yes, yes, yes, yes, yes.

Colin That's right.

Alex Yes, yes.

Colin Good, good.

Alex And you, dear.

Colin Of course, of course.

Alex I walked down past the houses under the catalpa and the boatmen's cottages past the club houses and the pubs, and the houseboats riding above the wall, and past the public lavatory and across the green and through the alleyway where there was another pub, till I got to the row of houses where you lived. It was late afternoon and I had come straight from work and I really wanted, well, to fuck you then, really, but you wanted to show me the river further upstream. Which you did indeed. All the houses seemingly getting grander the further we went. And you pointed out where various eminences had lived, none of whom of course I had heard of, until we lost the river in an alley where there was another little pub and a deserted mansion behind a wall and a factory and another pub into a smart terrace, where you had deduced that some character in Dickens must have lived. And out onto an esplanade of big houses with gardens across the way fronting the river, their grandeur emphasised by there being no more pubs or boathouses, just their various magnificences. And beyond the Eyot the river had flooded over the road, so that we could go no farther and missed seeing the churchyard further up, where more of the famous were apparently buried. And the sun was, was it, low in the sky and spreading red on the Surrey side, was it, as it always seemed to be in the late afternoon, down there, when I came to visit. And we came back to your room and I did indeed . . . well, yes . . . fuck you. And later, I remember, we could see that the tide had turned, by the reflection of the river in the ceiling above your bed.

Nicholas (*to Alex*) Tea?

Alex What?

Colin Do you want tea, tea?

Alex Do I want tea?

Nicholas I can make you some.

Alex No, no.

Nicholas Are you sure? Why are you laughing? It'll be alright, honestly.

Alex What?

Colin Are you sure? Tell me if you do.

Alex Yes, yes.

Nicholas Really. No trouble.

Colin Are you?

Nicholas Or we could finish our walk.

Colin I met you in the Partisan coffee house in Soho in . . .
oh up beyond . . . round by . . . beyond . . . down from
Kettner's and from Jimmy's, where we used sometimes to eat
and up from Chez Victor where we didn't eat, though I did
once years later. Up from Dean Street the little street that
leads into Soho Square. A singular and unremembered
marker of the post-war intellectual left or rather of
realignment after Suez and Hungary, I suppose. Where the
borscht and the cheesecake that it served was an indication
of its roots in the past, and its repudiation of the espresso
bars of the period a singular comment on the present. Where
you could take up a table all day, as far as I could see,
having bought one cup of coffee. Where, I suppose,
deliberate lack of any of conventional business practice, even
then, in the world even then, ensured quite soon its demise.
It suited you more than me in fact, who was too intimidated
to venture down to the basement where the chessboards
were and where were organised the Aldermaston marches.
Or upstairs where there was a library – for you were big in
NUS politics and had a room in the students' union in
Bloomsbury, in some kind of quid pro quo. Where you
sneaked me in at night and out early morning. For they were
less liberated days, and, though not exactly blokeish, race
and gender didn't figure in the picture – certainly not in the
Partisan where the dominant tone was male and
heterosexual, and queer was still the word. Though I always
sat with a pacifist lecturer in anthropology called Freda with
whom I went on the Aldermaston march – in the event
behind whichever banner would have us. Where on the first
one I remember, for some reason vividly, at Turnham Green,
a group during a halt . . . a group of bejeaned art students. It
seemed uniformly beautiful. Like a prefiguring of things, an
annunciation of what was to come, so many James Taylors
before their time. All with long soft hair falling in curls, it
seemed, and wispy beards. With the look of leaders of future

communes. Unnerving and alluring and something fascist. And after the march, to Freda's flat in Langham Place where she made soup, for some of the ragtag. Who I rarely bring to mind now.

Gareth is there.

Gareth (*to Colin*) Where shall we meet then?

Colin I don't know.

Gareth It's up to you.

Colin I don't know.

Gareth You say. I'm easy.

Colin Who do you mean?

Alex Better hurry up if he is coming then.

Gareth That would suit me fine.

Colin Who? Who?

Gareth Or we could meet on the steps. Wherever you like really.

Alex If he is.

Colin Who?

Gareth Would that be alright for you?

Alex You know.

Gareth I can use my union card.

Alex You know, you know.

Gareth What do you think?

Colin I don't.

Gareth Looking forward.

Alex Oh dear.

Gareth Or we could meet on the steps.

Colin The clientele of the Partisan was in the main older than us. Some of the men must had fought in the war or in Korea or Malaya or in Cyprus. Our memories of the war confused in the generality of childhood rather than anything consecutive. Your mother's anxiety at the sound of the siren. The air-raid shelter in the night. The barrage balloon in the park, the single Spitfire. Cod-liver oil and malt and the taste of government orange. The blackouts, the ration books, the Mickey Mouse gas mask, the damp towels and Paul Robeson and Uncle Joe and Popeye and Ernest Bevin and Carmen Miranda and Lord Woolton and Betty Grable and Alvar Lidell and the death of Bambi's mother.

Nicholas Nice.

Alex The river was going out and the sun was going down in a blaze.

Gareth Shall we go for some lunch?

Alex I was unnerved you know by that house when I first came there, where the hall was dark and the walls were white and there was no dining room but a kitchen converted, so that it was half modern and half quite else. With a big wooden table and benches to it at one end and a dresser covered with china and a collection of memorial plates to Gladstone and china dogs, and on the wall was a country clock that didn't work, and at the other end all more up to date. And with a newly built room extending out of it into the garden, where there was a Pither stove and a big reproduction of a bright abstract picture by Matisse made of coloured paper cut-outs, which then I couldn't see why . . . until explained . . . was called *The Snail*, which was the beginning of my cottoning on – as was learning to say Purcell, and contra versy. And a model sailing ship in a glass case among the *objets trouvés* on the bookcase. All designed by an architect who they knew of course, and living nearby of course. And yet in contrast upstairs, in the drawing room, the doors and dado were hand painted with gold cupids flanking the windows onto the balcony. And sconces in the walls, and above the fireplace a big carved wooden Renaissance picture frame with no picture it, and everywhere wooden floors and a very few rugs. And books like you'd never seen. I was a would-be city boy, just finished my national service, with a room in a flat off Bayswater Road landed through my Auntie Doris, furnished with carpets and sofas and wallpaper. And whatever irritated and unformed feelings I might have had about what that represented to me, it was what I was used to.

They won't let him bring the dog up here.

Colin Who, who?

Alex Will they?

Colin Who?

Alex Oh dear, mm. What's his name?

Colin I don't know.

Alex He won't be able to bring the dog.

Colin Who?

Alex What's his name? What's his name? What's his name?

Colin Shshsh.

Alex Oh dear.

Colin Shshsh.

Alex Oh dear.

Colin Who do you mean?

Alex makes a remembering sound as he thinks.

It's alright.

Alex Robert. Robert.

Colin Is it?

Alex Yes, yes.

Colin There we are.

Alex That house pictured for me a divide in the middle class. My father worked for Cable and Wireless. We were not long back from Rhodesia and my school, which was sponsored by a foundation set up to give boys like me an education that mimicked the poshest, had done its work insofar as it had landed me my job and ensured I could just about handle myself on my entry into upper-middle-class Bohemia.

Andrew is there.

Andrew Dad.

Nicholas How about Tuesday?

Andrew Dad.

Colin Oh good, you're here, are you? Is this him? This is him, isn't it? Look, he's here.

Alex What? What?

Gareth When's easy for you? You say. I'm fairly free.

Alex Who? Who?

Colin He was waiting for you.

Gareth You say.

Andrew How you doing, Dad? It's me, Dad.

Alex Yes. Yes.

Gareth How about Wednesday eight o'clock?

Andrew How are you then today, Dad?

Nicholas Seven-thirty then.

Andrew Dad?

Alex Yes, yes.

Colin He was worried.

Nicholas I can come straight from work.

Gareth Fine by me.

Andrew And how are you?

Colin I'm well. Are you? You've been here before, haven't you?

Gareth Can't wait.

Alex Have you come to see me then?

Andrew I have. I have.

Nicholas Tuesday, seven-thirty. I'm looking forward.

Alex They won't let you bring the dog up, you know . . .

Colin I did indeed see you across a room through a kind of blue about you and something smudged and rose-coloured and immediately attractive that revealed a gentle head boy hesitancy and an almost maternal concern. We walked into north London through the summer night in an ecstasy of talk from Soho through Bloomsbury and up past the Craven A factory and into Camden Town and an early morning fuck on Primrose Hill.

Alex Are you my son?

Andrew Yes, Dad.

Alex Yes, yes. Good, good.

Colin That's right.

Alex My son.

Colin Yes.

Alex Robert.

Andrew No, Dad. Andrew.

Alex Oh yes, Andrew.

Colin You see.

Alex Andrew. They won't let the dog up, Andrew.

Andrew No, Dad.

Alex Not Robert.

Andrew No, Dad.

Colin Yes.

Alex But it was all made easy by the kindness of your landlady, Muriel, who you knew because you had been at university with the son of the house. The father was a hotshot at the BBC and you were working for him. She the author of a highly regarded novel sequence, set in the pre-war Balkans and in London during the Blitz. I had never of course . . . And all out of print then. He, tall and plump and wore a battered old-fashioned tailor-made double-breasted suit and a club tie and a crumpled shirt and smoked like a chimney, and knew, it seemed, everyone and everything about everything. And their relationship flavoured by his patronising her. He once observed in my hearing that we all resemble our cars. He had an old Morgan and she drove a little battered Ford convertible, which made his comment, which he had directed at her, not the kindest. *I thought* he might be queer too, but he was in fact having an affair, which had only recently come to light, with a painter woman with the most alarming posh laugh, and eventually there was a divorce. And all that, you must remember, were not how things were then in St Albans.

My son, are you?

Andrew Yes, Dad, that's right.

Alex Good, good.

Andrew Yes. Andrew.

Alex Andrew.

Andrew Yes, Dad.

Colin That's right. You see.

Alex Andrew.

Colin Perhaps it was the ease of it that makes it difficult to access and then when it comes like sudden sunlight. I wasn't used for things to be so available, that hadn't as it were been earned. Things then seemed mostly always out of reach. And you made it easy, before I could put up a barrier or find some way of spoiling it. And the break-up so soon like the profligacy of the poor, the squandering of fine days. And in truth what happened between us was an aggregate of later encounters, in fact. Of really encounters and meetings over years. And for both of us then, at the beginning, there was our life, as they say, thus far. Mutually alienated is the truth of it. In your case a result I thought, in my text book way, of your mother's remoteness. Dutiful in every way but lacking the affection that you could so readily give. And then I realised quite soon that you would be incapable of being faithful. It was a position you took, a deal you cut. A statement of your autonomy. As if the price to be paid for your seeming otherwise an epitome of everything that was the norm. In every other way your seeming so good. The perfect son, the perfect pupil, the obvious head boy. But for all that a dedicated ram, needing, as it used to be said, to fuck anything that moved. And in my case there was fear of the stigma, then certainly, of effeminacy. Certainly as it was manifested by the boy you had been seeing at the time and had dumped. Though you, I think, in fairness, didn't feel you had dumped anyone, just added to them. For you were still seeing him when we met. He was easy with it, you said, but that was not the impression he gave me. Just putting up with it gracefully.

So in the end it was a reflection of two people's characters and temperaments. And . . . oh . . . youth . . . life through the fingers. But whenever we subsequently met, always between us, something . . . sophisticated in its way but wasteful nevertheless. It was as if, in truth, we accepted that we were, it was, disposable. But there was something secret kept between us always. And something superior in our attitude to what we had done or were doing. Unable for some reason to cut a deal or do what might have been better for us perhaps. And my continuing feeling of power that you always gave me whenever we met. Even in the days of your success. And almost acknowledging an inability to cut the necessary deal. And you took relationships as they came. As if they were the next train.

Nicholas Your eyes, for one.

Gareth Everything about you, in fact.

Nicholas Your smile.

Gareth Your eyes.

Nicholas You're beautiful.

Alex I realise now that that must have been when Muriel was writing the espionage novel which made a splash when it was first published just at the time that the Cambridge spies were first outed, because it was centred on its heroine's discovery – consequent upon her discovery of her husband's long-term adulterous affair – of his having been, without her knowing it, a Soviet agent all through their marriage and before. With the added piquancy of her real husband, your boss, having been widely thought to be suspect anyway because of his undergraduate communism. The book, you said, was really more a mordant take on middle-class life than a thriller. So that told me. The book's success caused a publisher that only published books by women to reissue her more famous books. And you made a television film about her, but not before she died. So. And indeed

when one of the last of the Cambridge spies was outed,
I realised that he had been given refuge from the press by a
man I had met in that house. Someone very unlikely, further
up, an absolute nancy art critic. And many, well most, were
like the adulterous lady artist and her husband who were
hardly more left wing than any member of the Liberal
Party. It was she who organised the carol singing at
Christmas when they went from house to house. Her very
tall daughter, Evadne, carrying a lantern.

Andrew sees that Colin and Alex are holding hands.

Andrew What's this then, Dad?

Alex What? What?

Nicholas You're invited to lunch on Sunday.

Andrew You don't want to do that, Dad.

Gareth I'm going to a meeting this evening. I don't know
that it would interest you. You're welcome to come.

Colin Don't.

Nicholas It'll be fine. Honestly. They won't bite you.

Gareth It's at the LSE.

Andrew takes Alex's hand away.

Andrew You don't want to be doing that, Dad.

Gareth Do you want to come? Might interest you.

Colin Don't.

Nicholas I'll meet you outside the Blue Anchor at one.

Gareth We could go out afterwards.

Andrew Dad.

Alex No. No.

Andrew No, Dad. Come on.

23

Gareth Jimmy's suit you?

Nicholas We could go to Kew.

Alex cries out.

Colin No, no. Stop it.

Nicholas Depends on the tide.

Gareth I'll pay. My grant is through.

Andrew No, come on. No, seriously. For crying out loud. What the fuck's this now, Dad?

Alex Robert.

Andrew No, Dad. Andrew, Andrew.

Colin That's right.

Nicholas Right.

Alex My son, Robert.

Andrew Andrew. Andrew.

Alex My son, Andrew.

Andrew laughs.

Andrew Oh fuck it.

Gareth Good.

Alex And she kept her many unpaid parking tickets in a bowl on the dresser and smoked Rothmans, and showed a tendency towards pyromania by making little fires in the ashtray. She was all of a period I suppose and wore trousers and much-laundered shirts and hair done and painted nails and wore a musky heavy dressy scent. She had a self-conscious melancholy, and my abiding memory of her is her washing up slowly behind the sink cigarette in mouth listening to us as we talked at the big table. And she loved you and she was very nice to me.

Clare is there.

Clare (*to Colin*) It's Clare, Uncle.

Colin Hello, Clare dear. I was asleep.

Clare How are you?

Gareth I like your room.

Clare How have you been?

Colin Well. Well.

Gareth Nice, very.

Nicholas Lot of stairs.

Clare Oh good. I've put some things in your room, Uncle. I'll not be long. I'm coming again on Thursday, okay?

Colin Good. Good.

Gareth Big. Nice.

Colin This is Alex's son.

Clare We meet again.

Nicholas You can see the park.

Andrew Yes.

Clare Did you drive?

Andrew I did.

Clare You found a space this time.

Andrew I did.

Clare Lucky you then.

Gareth Very nice.

Andrew You?

Clare I came by bus. Didn't want to risk it.

Andrew Six of one. I could probably give you a lift, you know.

Nicholas Through the chimneys.

Clare Right out of your way.

Gareth Look, you can walk straight into the garden.

Andrew Not necessarily.

Clare How?

Andrew I can go under the flyover.

Clare Oh.

Gareth North London, eh?

Andrew Very near to where you are. Anyway.

Clare (*giving Colin a packet*) I brought you this, Uncle. I hope it's what you wanted.

Gareth Lilac.

Colin How are you, dear?

Clare I'm well.

Nicholas Plane trees are they?

  Colin makes a sound of approval.

Clare Is that what you wanted?

Alex And you ribbed me mercilessly about my enthusiasm for rock and roll. You said the music I liked was a betrayal of its own roots as, you said, so much of America was implicitly a betrayal of its roots. Which was rich of you really since it interested you enough to make a film about it. The first in fact of any distinction, which still gets an occasional showing at the BFI. You maintained that the serpent had entered the garden when Elvis Presley released 'It's Now Or Never', which Mario Lanza had made famous.

And of course a notable hit. And I remember a kind of bowing of the head when he did, and thinking 'uh-oh'. And I suppose as I speak there must be some old banker, retired to Switzerland doing his yoga and listening to his Bob Dylan records and so on.

Andrew What about this? What do you make of this?

Clare What?

Andrew This.

Clare What?

Andrew They're holding hands.

Clare I see.

Andrew Oh, okay. Well what do you make of it?

Clare I don't make anything of it.

Andrew Fuck. This now.

Clare What?

Andrew Sorry, sorry. But it can't be right, can it?

Clare 'Right'?

Andrew Suitable then, sensible, sorry. Is it suitable, whatever? What should we do?

Clare What do you mean, what should we do?

Andrew (*head in hands*) Fuck. Better when he wouldn't eat.

Clare Oh, do you think, really?

Andrew Oh come off it. Yes. No. Much the same. How long has this been going on then?

   Clare laughs.

Clare 'Going on'?

Andrew What?

Clare Really. I've no idea.

Andrew Well are you happy with it?

Clare Happy! Come on.

Andrew Well.

Clare It's an expression of friendship. They're friends. And it's not our business anyway.

Andrew Well I'm not happy with it. It's embarrassing. He's my dad.

Clare I don't find it embarrassing. Do you really?

Andrew I don't believe you.

Clare Honestly I don't. Not expected perhaps, certainly.

Andrew I don't find it funny. It's a bit of a surprise you know to find your father holding another bloke's hand.

Clare Yes.

Andrew Part of the condition, is it? Is that what you think is it?

Clare They're just holding hands you know. Chill, someone might say.

Andrew Some might say. He doesn't know what he's doing. What would he think?

Clare There we are.

Andrew Don't be smart.

Clare But that's it, isn't it?

Andrew What?

Clare Well, what would he think? And we'll never know. I shouldn't look any further, you know. No good looking for comprehension, you know. Looking for sense, as we understand it anyway. I don't think it's worth speculating.

Andrew What do you mean? Speculating. On what? Who's speculating?

Clare Nothing, nothing.

Andrew Speculating, what?

Clare And what are you going to do – separate them?

Andrew Fuck it. Fuck it. Fuck it. Sorry, sorry. Embarrassed, I suppose. It's my dad.

Clare Come on now.

Andrew Are you always like this?

Clare Like what?

Andrew So fucking reasonable.

Clare Really.

Andrew So cool, so . . . head girl.

Clare Oh, please.

Andrew No. Fine in other circumstances. Attractive in fact.

Clare Oh, honestly.

Andrew It is.

Clare Please.

Andrew And you don't find this . . .?

Clare They've each found a friend. He's found a friend. Isn't it a good thing? It's a good thing, isn't it?

Alex But my feelings of enjoyment and, well, liberation that the music gave me were such that defied scrutiny and analysis. And yet I always referred to you in my mind from then on. A sort of cultural check-up. My father said of sex, when he got very old, that he'd reached a time, he said, when he'd sooner have bacon and eggs. So me now and music. And I find refuge in Jerry Lee Lewis, who you claimed from the beginning was the real deal. A startling juxtaposition, you and Jerry Lee Lewis. And listening to The Crystals singing 'And then he kissed me' reminding me of a time when my alternate sex fantasies involved Russ Tamblyn or Brigitte Bardot.

Gareth *Aidez L'Espagne*, mm.

Colin You were looking at a poster on my wall.

Gareth Wow.

Colin I explained that my landlady had been in Spain.

Gareth Wow. Your landlady.

Colin My landlady, Ursula, who you had just met.

Gareth Ursula.

Colin Ursula. She drove an ambulance.

Gareth Wow. Did she . . .?

Colin She worked with refugees. Hence Jenno and Maria.

Gareth Really.

Colin Jenno and Maria, the Hungarian couple who lived upstairs.

Gareth I see.

Colin Years before that, Russia in the civil war.

Gareth She couldn't have.

Colin I don't see why she would lie.

Gareth Blimey. Formidable.

Colin She is.

Gareth After the revolution.

Colin I suppose.

Gareth Those were the days.

Colin She was your age.

Gareth Formidable.

Alex All over London, large and small, there were houses like that in terraces like that. Only their often unexpected location giving the lie to their being in Hampstead or Chelsea. Or Hampstead and Chelsea as then they were. With owners for whom Kensington held no charms, and who had confidence enough in their own taste and money enough of course to exercise it. And often just removed enough from poverty.

Colin But I didn't share your enthusiasm for Ursula's rather uncompromising Quaker personality, which was rather mean-spirited of me I think now. Something dispassionate about her that I was still too provincial to easily understand. But she liked to have a student in the house among the other deserving, and I landed my room through the kindness of my head of department. Part of the bunce that comes with good A levels and the right university. I could never be easy with Ursula's apparent compulsion to disagree emphatically with an opinion just when it might have been more comfortable for everyone if she had taken the more tactful option. A characteristic that was, I take it, innate, as well as resulting from the struggle she had had to do what she did when she did it, in a field in which she was such a pioneer. I have an image of her in her drawing room sitting magisterially among all the objects that reflected her travels, pouring tea and offering Fuller's walnut cake and opinion. She was one of the independently minded women who the BBC called on then to pronounce on issues that reflected their experience. All with a striking command of the language and in accents that have completely disappeared. Violet Bonham Carter and Catherine Bramwell-Booth, Vita Sackville-West, Barbara Wootton, Edith Sitwell, Ivy Compton-Burnett and so on. Muriel Bradbrook, Marghanita Laski et al. Beatrice Webb and

Virginia Woolf only missing by having gone before. And, in the imagination, accompanied by Kathleen Ferrier singing 'Blow the Wind Southerly'.

Alex We first met, you know, in fact at a New Year's Eve party in Islington given by a Scottish doctor I knew through his brother with whom I had been in school. It purported to be fancy dress and he was dressed in full Highland fig and you were dressed as a choir boy which I thought was rather asking for it. And I was in my city suit and a pirate's hat and a beard on elastic, which I suppose was a signal of its own you'd say, so fuck off. And among the others dressed in perked-up city suits and more liberated outfits like yours, I remember, sitting on a sofa, a very young quite pretty theology student from Bristol who was having none of it, as far as dress was concerned, and was carrying a copy of *Mein Kampf* for some reason, and was being rather ostentatiously shunned by the other guests. Except for you who sat with him, I supposed, in support of the open society, which I thought was stylish of you. Though I must confess, however, that I was also entertaining thoughts about both of you of a less high-minded nature.

Andrew Should we speak to the whatever of this place?

Clare About what?

Andrew Come off it. About this.

Clare Oh come on. It's company for them, can't you see? It's nice for them. Please don't make a fuss.

Andrew What do the powers that be make of this though, seriously?

Clare I hope they don't make anything of it. Look, there's a woman here you know who harms herself routinely. Last time I was here she had cut a cross on her head. I think we should be grateful. You've heard the noise that man makes when he gets agitated sometimes. Small mercies.

Andrew And you're not concerned about this though?

Clare I'm really not.

Andrew What would he think?

Clare We know what he thinks.

Andrew Not him. Him. Oh fuck.

Clare And we'll never know.

Colin Come on, tie it to the tree.

Gareth What?

Colin There was a willow growing out of the bank lapped by the water.

Gareth What?

Colin We were on the river in Richmond.

Gareth Why?

Colin Go on.
   You tied it.

Gareth That suit Boss?

Colin Funny. Yes.

Gareth See.

Colin Clever boy. Come on.

Gareth What?

Colin Let's go in.

Gareth What?

Colin Come on.

Gareth No . . .

Colin Yes.

Gareth No trunks, for one.

Colin Come on.
We undressed and slid into the water.

Gareth Oo.

Colin Yeah.

Gareth Christ.

Colin There we are, lovely. Watch the weeds.
And we swam and floated and splashed until . . .

Gareth Oh Christ, look.

Colin What?

Gareth Look.

Colin There was a motorboat coming upstream. You scrambled to get out.

Gareth Oh fuck.

Colin And slipped on the bank.

Gareth Bugger.

Colin Idiot.
And you stood under the willow, your hands cupped over your cock and balls like Adam in a painting, while I ducked under the water until the boat had passed.

Alex I associate the moon landing with Muriel, not just because we watched it in her house but because of her absolute disapproval of it – a crossing of the line that she didn't want to discuss. As if it was profane, a sacrilege, the ultimate going too far – this fly-tipping into the universe. And among the many poems Muriel knew and could quote from – which she said she learned when she drove a tractor on a farm in Hampshire during the war – was one which she quoted that night about the moon being like a dying lady. 'Like a dying lady, lean and pale.'

34

Colin *L'Après-midi d'un* lock forward.

Alex Why am I rehearsing this all this now? That's forgotten for years at time. Gone for good. My youth, my Eden. And you who had given it to me.

Nicholas I can get tickets easy. We can drive. Muriel will lend us her car. It'll be great. We can stay the night.

Alex You haven't brought the dog, Robert?

Andrew No, Dad.

Clare Missing his dog.

Andrew I suppose so. I don't know why.

Clare No? What was it?

Andrew Labrador. Bruno.

Clare Mm. Nice.

Andrew I can't think why he still features.

Clare How come?

Andrew He must be dead twenty years.

Nicholas Come on. It'll be great.

Colin And my anger was such on the night of the Cuban Missile Crisis that I remember, after having spent the evening with Freda, being unable to sleep, lying in bed with the curtains open looking out through the French doors into the garden into the moonlight until eventually I had to get up and walked up to Parliament Hill Fields in a blank fury.

Nicholas We can drive back or stay the night.

Colin Such was my anger.

Nicholas What do you say?

Alex I sometimes think that I've only reached the point that most people reach when they are forty, as far as everyday competence goes.

35

Colin My stay in north London was brief, since soon after our meeting I landed a residency in a settlement house in Lambeth, and then a job in the children's department. And that was it. South of the river to this day. But your enthusiasm for the city north of Bloomsbury was sealed, and later when you landed a job at UCL you bought a flat in Camden just at the right time. For you were canny with money, arising, you said, from your peasant roots in the Welsh borders in the farm your mother still managed – your father having died a couple of years before we met.

Alex My memory is getting worse by the day.

Nicholas It's going to be another beautiful day.

Colin What's his name, what's his name, dammit . . .

Alex And if I recall it as a time before the Fall I increasingly think that was the case and certainly I remember much of it better than I do day to day at present, such is the state of memory. And of course I'd had girlfriends – referred to by you as my unfortunate tendency when I made Jack the Lad observations of pretty women. But otherwise sanguine. And nothing was declared between us either and it became a rather masculine accommodation, at least on the surface. But underneath, something buried by both of us. But principally, overriding affection and friendship and love really, and admiration, certainly by me. And anyway what the fuck did we know of good sense. We were not of an age or temperament to think of consequences, or up to the virtue of addressing things.

Colin And there was too an immature melancholy that coloured my response to your affection . . . love . . . Too easily obtained perhaps for someone of my temperament. Too easily got. This is it? Is it? Is it? The parity in our relation, the balance. How come? And the break-up in Green Park, sitting on the green sward in the sunlight beyond all the trees. Its anonymous grandeur also perhaps meaning that I've never sat in it since.

Andrew He was a picture dealer.

Clare Was he? Really.

Andrew Difficult to imagine now.

Clare No, no.

Andrew Difficult to think they could do anything, either of them.

Clare Better not to think more than is useful perhaps.

Andrew Yes. I don't think I have the wherewithal. The temperament for this, if I'm to be honest.

Clare No.

Andrew True.

Clare Did he work in London? I suppose he must have done.

Andrew They had a gallery in the World's End.

Clare They?

Andrew Yes. With money from my grandfather, my mother's father. Soon after they were married.

Clare Your mother with us?

Andrew She certainly is. She lives in Sussex.

Clare Oh.

Andrew With her husband and their children.

Clare Oh.

Andrew Grown-up children in fact.

Clare Does she visit?

Andrew She most definitely doesn't.

Clare And the gallery now?

Andrew Oh it didn't survive the crash I'm afraid. My brother Robert was running it by then and he'd just taken it in a new direction and it was promising well in fact, but trade fell off and he couldn't service the loan he'd secured to expand the business. And that was it, I'm afraid.

Clare Oh dear. I'm sorry.

Colin A couple of hops up the university ladder, and you became – your romantic life excepted – undistinguishable from any other ambitious young don in a sports coat sitting on college committees and interesting yourself in student welfare. Taking foreign students to concerts and the theatre and to look at the Burghers of Calais in the Victoria Tower Gardens. And then came the partner and the house. The partner Christopher was, is, a lawyer working then for the university. And something of a doormat it seemed to me. Well, complaisant, compliant then. I don't know why I'm being uncharitable. It must have suited him since you and he had similar social aspirations, and the house you eventually bought was of course in Hampstead. And social life, outside work and its obligations, became exclusively gay.

Alex And you encouraged me to quit my city job to take up the offer of work from a dealer in prints and drawings who had a tiny gallery in his flat in Hans Place, and who I had of course met in Muriel's house, and who said he could use my rudimentary accounting skills in spite of my inexperience. And I developed an aptitude, a skill for the ferreting and dealing and blarney required for the trade. Remember things were not quite so Courtauld Institute then, and I found an interest, more a passion really, in the graphic artists of the late years of the nineteenth century. I once found a sketch I believed was by Van Gogh, copied from the engraving of a chair in a graphic magazine, which I believed was a study for a later painting, but couldn't persuade the powers. Only to find much later of course, about ten years ago now, that I had been right since it had by then been authenticated.

Colin And by then you had added a young Irishman called Tommy to the mix, who soon became a fixture like an official mistress. Christopher more suitable for best I suppose . . .

Alex And I once found, in a bundle bought at a country sale, an etching by Whistler of the river just by Muriel's house which I sold to the husband of the painter woman. I don't know to what extent all this had an effect on what happened then. How much a new perspective led me to bite on the apple when it was offered.

Colin I can remember one of a group in a pub where you sometimes drank – a tall man with curling lips wearing a foulard and looking like Don John in an amateur production of *Much Ado About Nothing*. A sort of period cliché and a Yorkshire contrarian to boot and absolutely of the time and not at all my *tasse de*, but you were always more sanguine about people than I.

Alex Yesterday I put the electric kettle on the hob.

Colin And I remember that whenever you tried to vary the sports coat and flannels, in which you looked absolutely as you should, with the more fashionable gear of the time, the result was usually disastrous.

Gareth takes something from a Take Six bag.

Oh dear.

Gareth Don't you think?

Colin No, I don't.

Gareth No?

Colin No. Believe me. No.

Gareth You're the boss. You know . . . Really?

Colin Really.

Gareth What about these?

Colin What are they?

Gareth Bell bottoms.

Colin Trust me.

Gareth Anyway how are you? Did you get the grant? You weren't feeling so bright last time, the bastards. Did they give you the money?

Colin Yes.

Gareth Sweetheart, you're so good. That's what it is.

Takes something else out of the bag.

This? No?

Colin I must look at my will.

Clare He always insisted that he was just a social worker, but that's not the whole story by any means. He was a regular fixture on government committees dealing with family policy, and particularly concerned with issues surrounding children in care, about which he wrote extensively. Articles, reports, two books. He was active until quite recently as a trustee of a fund, which awards a scholarship in memory of an old friend of his who died of Aids.

Colin All these books. What about all these books?

Clare And I've brought some things for you to look at, Uncle, before I go.

Colin Thank you.

Clare Look, there's a postcard from Freda in New York.

She takes a postcard from the bundle of papers she's handing to him.

Colin Freda.

Clare Yes, Freda.

Colin Oh, Freda.

Clare She lives in America now.

Colin She does.

Clare She says she's coming over at Easter and will come to see you.

Colin Good.

Colin shows the postcard to Alex.

Look.

Alex What?

Colin Look, nice. See?

Alex Oh, yes.

Colin America.

Clare And I've said you won't be going to the trust meeting again this year, Uncle.

Colin Oh yes.

Andrew Haven't you got power of attorney?

Clare I have. But still. You know. For form's sake I suppose . . . He's got security of tenure of the little house he's lived in since he first moved to Lambeth. It's part of a settlement under the patronage of the Bishop of London, which they want to develop, and they are keen to know what the chances are of his moving back.

Andrew Are there any?

Clare I don't think any. So. But you know.

Andrew No, I know.

Clare You?

Andrew We sold the flat eighteen months ago.

Colin And later, much later, we met for dinner when I saw you had for some reason acquired a moustache which made you look very seedy I thought, and told you so. And when we met the next evening outside the Wigmore Hall where we had agreed to go to a piano recital, you'd shaved it off, you said by mistake.

Colin You can't do this.

Gareth What?

Colin Shave off your moustache because I don't like it.

Gareth It was a mistake. It was a mistake.

Colin Oh yes.

Gareth It was.

Colin Worse. Unconscious mistake is worse. What did Christopher say?

Gareth It's a mistake. I did it automatically when I was shaving. And you didn't like it.

Colin I certainly didn't. That's beside the point.

Gareth I didn't mean to do it. I didn't, honestly.

Colin Oh yes.

Gareth And anyway you're always right.

Colin Schumann.

Alex She had the figure for whom dolly-bird clothes could have been designed. As if the manufacturer had her in mind when they made them up, for whom the mini skirt was bespoke. Legs up to here, blonde as blonde, something about her that was both maiden and imp. Innocent and alluring. Something woodland almost about her. An old boyfriend of hers, a posh bounder in hippy disguise of a type that cut swathes through the ranks of young upper-class maidens then, told me that recalling her phone number gave him a

hard-on. The deed was done at a rock festival on the Isle of
Wight to which you wouldn't come because of work. After a
certain amount of drug taking and drink. And she was bit of
a prize you know, feeble as that sounds. And I was by now
so utterly, so overwhelmed by my feelings for her that
suddenly it was as if all the questions were answered. As if
the puzzle had been solved, something had been sorted, out
of my hands, all anxiety dissolved. And I knew it might be
hard for you and I couldn't do anything about it. I was
incapable of any other course of action. And, as if
automatically, quite brutally reverted to type – made worse
because, of course, part of me knew that's what I was doing.
As if in the grip of something mercilessly conventional, and
as if all the home counties were behind me, practically
referring to custom and practice. And also pissed off that
you couldn't get it and what was there to say – 'This is it,
I'm sorry but there we are.' Practically – 'I think you'll agree
with me,' and reduced to saying that 'I don't have to justify
myself to you, you know.'

Nicholas You smug cunt.

Alex Well I don't.

Nicholas Oh please.

Alex Oh come on.

Nicholas What come on?

Alex Did you never think?

Nicholas Think what?

Alex Fuck off, Nick. You never, never thought?

Nicholas What?

Alex Oh come off it. You can't have thought, can you . . .

Nicholas What?

Alex Oh dear. Christ. Can't you understand?

Nicholas Don't whine as well.

Alex This is how things are, Nick.

Nicholas I'm not doubting it.

Alex Don't be like that.

Nicholas Like what?

Alex Oh come on. Don't. Please.

Nicholas What?

Alex Well. I'm sorry.

Nicholas Yes.

Alex It's how it is, don't you see. Oh fuck. I'm sorry. This is how things are now.

Nicholas She belongs on the top of a Christmas tree.

Alex What? Fuck off. Just fuck off.

Nicholas Well it's true.

Alex We can still be friends, can't we?

Nicholas What? Oh Christ. What?

Alex You're my dearest friend.

Nicholas That's nice.

Alex I can't see how you can't see.
    I couldn't see how you couldn't see.

Nicholas Really.

Alex Well I can't help it.

Nicholas I realise that.

Alex Well.

Nicholas What?

Alex Oh dear.

Nicholas Well what?

Alex This is bloody awful.

Nicholas The smugness of it.

Alex I'm really sorry. Can't you understand?

Nicholas No.

Alex That was the last time I saw of you, to speak to at least. Once later at Muriel's funeral when you smiled and didn't speak. The last I heard you were teaching at a university in California.

Andrew You know we once went to the showing of a film by a friend of his at the BFI, some of which was shot in a house on the river belonging to family friends, and where my father met my mother. My word but they were . . . what . . . you know . . . on trend.

Clare Were they?

Andrew My mother had a framed invitation to a party they went to at that time hanging on the wall in the kitchen. Handmade on gold card with very bold period lettering instructing the guests to dress caj but fab.

Clare Very . . . on trend.

Andrew I think, you know, that she used to go out with the BFI film chap before my father came on the scene, which I think upset the applecart.

Clare Dear. Is she much changed now?

Andrew She's very much the plump country lady, you know, now, surrounded by rescue dogs.

Colin And once we met by chance when someone was giving me a bad time and I was feeling low.

Gareth Poor love. What a cunt.

Colin Yes.
    And went for a drink

Gareth Well for what it's worth, you know . . .

Colin What?

Gareth I still fancy you, for what it's worth.

Colin You shouldn't, you know.

Gareth I know. I know. Still I do. I'm afraid. What'll you have?

Nicholas What is it? What is it? Tell me, you can tell me. Fuck it, Alex, why this now? What have I done? What is it?

Alex 'And like a dying lady, lean and pale, who totters forth wrapped in a gauzy veil.'

Nicholas Tell me.

Clare I'll have to go quite soon you know. I've got to go to this trust meeting up in Bedford Square.

Andrew I have a meeting.

Clare You said. What about this? What are you suggesting we do? We'll have to resolve it you know. They've asked to share a room.

Andrew What? What do you mean? Oh Christ.

Clare Don't say 'Where's it going to end?' please.

Andrew Ho, ho. What do they say?

Clare They're fine with it. They have to be certain that we are.

Andrew Oh.

Clare We'll have to tell them. I said I'd see them on my way out. I have to go now, Uncle dear.

Colin Yes, yes.

Andrew Hang on, hang on.

Colin And it wasn't as if you took the libertarian route exactly, except implicitly, or that you were big on the virtues of Ludwig von Mises. I suppose it was inevitable thinking of you now. Something pragmatic in you. Times change, you implied when I took exception to your seeming new, I thought suspect, allegiances, with the rueful look you had and your sweet shrug and air of good-natured complacency, as if you been naughty again, as if you found a new boyfriend. And when I found you were acting in some advisory capacity on some economic matter or other to the SDP, it was a bit of a facer I must say.

Gareth Well you know . . . appropriate to the times.

Clare You'll have to make up your mind you know.

Gareth Don't look at me like that . . . Don't hit me.

Colin Honestly.

Gareth I know, I know.

Colin I don't know that you do.

Gareth Oh come on, come on.

Andrew Oh fuck it. Sellavee.

Clare What?

Andrew Sellavee. (*Laughs. Then, to Alex.*) Sellavee, Dad.

Clare What?

Andrew It's what Harry, my parents' odd-job man and driver at the gallery, used to say. Whatever the circumstances, however bad. 'Oh, sellavee.' Your house had burned down. 'Oh, sellavee.' We loved him.

Clare I'll square it with them then.

Colin It wasn't as if I thought that what we believed in in those days should or could be an ever-fixèd mark, or that your views should be unchanging. And I took what was a more practical view of things then, by reason of my work. I remember quite clearly your superior reminder that the women working in the Bangladesh sweat shops were replicating the lives of women in the Lancashire mills of the 1840s, with reference to the women I was working with, and, for some reason, to our mothers. While I, who fancied myself as working at the coal face, welcomed the new availability of cheap children's clothing. And sceptical of words from on high that seemed to sneer at the benefits of a plentiful supply of clean underclothes and towels. And all this was generational. For the people who protested with us in Grosvenor Square were in truth more concerned with individual freedoms than ever they were with social justice. And wars happen and banks crash. Which is why perhaps America so suited you when you went, first for seminars and conferences and then to New York on sabbatical for a year.

Clare Right, I must go.

Colin Just at exactly the wrong time for a young attractive promiscuous homosexual.

Andrew And he's got a hospital appointment next week.

Clare Oh dear. I know. How do you manage?

Andrew My daughter, Issie, comes with me. She's very good with him. And Robert's children and my sister-in-law.

Clare What's the prognosis?

Andrew Could be better.

Clare Oh.

Andrew Not good, I'm afraid.

Colin And then you died and I didn't.

48

Clare I take it, do I . . .?

Andrew What?

Clare Robert . . .

Andrew Oh.

Clare Sorry.

Andrew Yes.

Clare Oh dear, I hadn't thought.

Andrew No, why would you?

Colin We hadn't seen each other or spoken for over a year. More . . . when quite by chance I met Trevor, the chap who you were going out with when we first met, and who was still in touch with you, who told me how ill you were.

Clare I'm so sorry.

Andrew Yes.

Colin And when I came to visit you in hospital I found that your condition was even worse than I had been led to expect, because you had lost the ability to speak, as if you had suffered a stroke. And you communicated by intention since you had lost none of your intelligence, and you produced a version of speech by making sounds equivalent to the words you wanted to say, and between us we managed some understanding by me making a running translation and you indicating yes or no. Whether it made any sense in any conventional meaning of the word didn't matter, and we managed somehow to act as if it wasn't an obstacle.

Clare How . . .

Andrew He couldn't deal with losing the business is the truth, and I think he didn't have the wherewithal to deal with it because he'd never known failure before. Not that he hadn't worked hard you know, struggled, Robert, but the loss of what had been after all Dad's creation was too much for him I think.

Colin And when I left you I had only feelings of relief of having escaped.

Andrew He learned, you see, all the backstage tricks of the trade from Dad and from Harry who he'd helped in the school holidays since forever. And then university and the Courtauld Institute and a reputation for knowing what he was about, and articles in the posh journals ensured, you know, that he was pretty damn competent all round. He may not perhaps have had Dad's flair. That may be true. But it was as if losing the gallery was a blow to his very self. Must have been. He was never good at losing, but then he so rarely lost.

Clare Oh dear.

Colin And your condition deteriorated very quickly, and a couple of days later Tommy, the Irish boy, rang me to say that things were critical, and I put off going for hours not wanting to face what I could hardly believe was happening. But when I did go in I found that you looked as if you were sleeping only and they left me with you for a while and I sat by your bed holding your hand, and I remembered how fair and white your skin had been and how broad your shoulders were still under the single sheet that was covering you, I supposed to keep you cool. And how useless regret was, and how awful was this grief.

Clare What happened? I don't understand.

Andrew He simply lost it I'm afraid, you know, to the booze and to drugs and all that goes.

Colin And you died that night.

Clare Oh dear.

Andrew By which time he'd left his wife who he'd known since we were teenagers for a younger woman of course, and that didn't last. Though not before she had a child and he was mostly drunk by then.

Clare How?

Andrew He crashed his car on the motorway going to visit my mother.

Clare Oh no.

Colin And that was it then, all over.

Andrew In other circumstances he might have recovered, but his system was shot by that time and sepsis set in and they induced a coma, the better to be able to treat him, and put him on life support, but he was too wrecked by that stage and didn't benefit from the drugs they were giving, till it became clear that to all intents and purpose his body had shut down, and they advised turning the machine off.

Clare Were you there?

Andrew I was.

Clare How terrible.

Andrew I was there and Dad was there and my mother was, and after that my mother removed herself from us even more.

Colin The funeral was in Hampstead. Full Anglican and fine except the vicar called you Garry at one point. And there were touching tributes from Michael and Tommy and one of your colleagues in the university, and they played 'Träumerei' from *Kinderszenen* which fixed me. Then Highgate Cemetery of course, and you were buried not far in fact from Ursula, which was comforting, and no distance from Karl Marx so you know . . . and drinks after at the house where the mourners fell into two groups. One in the kitchen where was congregated a faithful handful of old boyfriends, among whom I was the most senior except for Trevor. Your mother was in the sitting room with the more regular mourners, imperious as ever but more relaxed than I had known her in the brief meetings we'd had when I visited. I learned she'd come up to help nurse you at the end, poor woman, and according to Tommy, things had become resolved between you. And I have wondered since if there was any provision made for Tommy since Christopher would, I'm sure, have got the house.

Clare I can't think how you managed.

Andrew I'm afraid I didn't.

Clare Oh.

Andrew No.

Clare How so?

Andrew I practically followed suit as far the booze was concerned I'm afraid.

Clare But not to any extent I see.

Andrew Well it wrecked my marriage and, if you can call it that, my business very nearly.

Clare What's that?

Andrew I'm in the book trade.

Clare But you have evidently come through. Haven't you?

Andrew Hope so, yes.

Clare Hence your meeting, I take it.

Andrew Indeed.

Colin And later there was a memorial at St George's Bloomsbury. Very university, full of academic toffs and ex-students. You had not long been made an associate professor. And a reception after in the Senate House to which I didn't go. I went to lunch with Trevor in the Gay Hussar.

Nicholas What time will you be free then?

Clare I must go I'm afraid now, Uncle. Is that okay? Or I'll be late for my appointment.

Gareth I have to get this essay finished.

Colin Yes, dear. Bye-bye then, dear. Bye-bye.

Nicholas Well just give me an idea.

Andrew And I mustn't be long.

Gareth When I've handed it in.

Nicholas Will you want to eat?

Clare I'm coming in to see you again later on in the week, is that okay?

Gareth And after that I intend to get pissed, care to join me?

Colin Yes, yes, dear.

Clare Where's my bag?

Nicholas I don't know.

Andrew Will you be coming again this day next week?

Clare I will.

Andrew Would you like a lift?

Nicholas Where then?

Clare Isn't it right out of your way?

Andrew Not really, it's quite easy if I don't go over the flyover.

Gareth Meet you there about seven in The Ship.

Clare Really?

Nicholas About eight then. Okay? Okay?

Andrew Really.

Clare Well in that case thank you. Otherwise three buses . . . Thank you.

Andrew There we are. That was not so bad, was it?

Clare Oh. Really.

Alex We were sitting on the balcony in our underwear drinking tea, watching the river go out and the sun go down in a blaze.

Nicholas Nice.

Alex And I realised how utterly without guile you were.

Nicholas It's getting dark.

Alex Yes. We'd better go in.

Nicholas Not yet.

Alex It's getting cold. You're shivering, sweetheart, come on.

Clare kisses Colin.

Clare Bye-bye then, dear.

Colin Bye-bye.

Clare (*to Alex*) Bye-bye.

Colin (*to Alex*) Say bye-bye.

Alex And we went back to my little room in Bayswater.

Gareth In the morning light.

Andrew Dad.

Alex Bye-bye.

Andrew I would say we could go for a drink.

Clare Can't you be trusted, you think?

Andrew Something like that. Should be by now, don't you think? Perhaps. What do you think?

Clare Not a decision for me.

Andrew The cards always so close to your chest?

Colin I realise I have no photograph of you.

Clare Why do you say that?

Andrew I haven't even gathered what it is you do.

Clare No.

Alex When I could fuck you without fear then.

Andrew He's lucky he's got you, you know.

Clare You think?

Andrew I do.

Nicholas You don't know how much.

Clare Really?

Colin And I haven't kept any of your letters.

Andrew Yes.

Clare If only you knew. I really must go. See you next week.

She goes.

Alex Yes.

Colin She's gone.

Andrew I'm going too now, Dad.

Alex Is that what you think. Is it really?

Nicholas I don't understand.

Andrew Going now, Dad, or I'll be late for my meeting, okay?

Alex My fault.

Colin Something missing in me, is it?

55

Gareth It's up to you, you know. It is.

Alex And what is character?

Nicholas Is it my fault? Is it always?

Colin What we make of it?

Andrew Issie and I are coming to take you to the doctor on Thursday. Okay? Okay?

Alex Yes, yes.

Colin Is that what it is? While I've got my wits about me.

Andrew (*to Colin*) Bye-bye then.

Colin Bye-bye. (*To Alex.*) Say bye-bye.

Alex Muriel became a dying lady, lean and pale.

Gareth Sweetheart.

Colin Andrew.

Nicholas My life.

Alex Yes.

Andrew That's right, Andrew. Bye-bye.

   Andrew goes.

Alex He's gone.

Colin Yes, nice boy . . . Andrew.

Nicholas Sh.

Gareth Sh

Nicholas What?

Gareth What?

Nicholas Sh, they'll hear you.

Gareth Who, who? Fuck.

Nicholas Quiet.

Gareth I've got such a big hard-on.

Nicholas Don't.

Gareth Come on.

Nicholas Stop it.

Gareth Shshhs.

Nicholas Don't put the light on.

Colin Dinner soon, dear, yes?

Alex Yes?

Colin Yes.

Alex Good, good.

Colin Hungry.

Alex Hungry. Hungry.

Colin Good.

Nicholas Your eyes, for one.

Gareth Everything about you in fact.

Nicholas Your smile.

Gareth Your eyes.

Nicholas You're beautiful.

Alex kisses Colin on the cheek.

Alex Nice.

Colin Yes.

Alex Yes.

Colin Yes.